CLASSIC WISD

Today's Questions. Timeless Answers.

Looking for time-tested guidance for the dilemmas of the spiritual life? Find it in the company of the wise spiritual masters of our Catholic tradition.

Christ in Our Midst: Wisdom from Caryll Houselander

Comfort in Hardship: Wisdom from Thérèse of Lisieux

Courage in Chaos: Wisdom from Francis de Sales

Inner Peace: Wisdom from Jean-Pierre de Caussade

Intimacy in Prayer: Wisdom from Bernard of Clairvaux

Life's Purpose: Wisdom from John Henry Newman

Path of Holiness: Wisdom from Catherine of Siena

Peace in Prayer: Wisdom from Teresa of Avila

Secrets of the Spirit: Wisdom from Luis Martinez

A Simple Life: Wisdom from Jane Frances de Chantal

Solace in Suffering: Wisdom from Thomas à Kempis

Strength in Darkness: Wisdom from John of the Cross

Intimacy in Prayer

CLASSIC WISDOM COLLECTION

Intimacy in Prayer

Wisdom from Bernard of Clairvaux

Compiled and with a Foreword by Ephrem Arcement, OSB

Pauline

BOOKS & MEDIA

Boston

Library of Congress Cataloging-in-Publication Data

Intimacy in prayer : wisdom from Bernard of Clairvaux / compiled and with a foreword by Ephrem Arcement, OSB.

    p. cm. -- (Classic wisdom collection)

  Includes bibliographical references.

  ISBN-13: 978-0-8198-3714-1

  ISBN-10: 0-8198-3714-8

  1. Spirituality--Catholic Church. 2. Prayer--Catholic Church. 3. Bernard, of Clairvaux, Saint, 1090 or 91-1153. 4. Spiritual life--Catholic Church. I. Arcement, Ephrem, editor of compilation.

  BX2350.65.I58 2013

  248.3'2--dc23

2012049866

Scripture quotations are transcribed from the original translations of Bernard of Clairvaux's works.

Excerpts from *The Divine Comedy, Paradiso* by Dante Alighieri and translated by Henry Wadsworth Longfellow.

English translation of Bernard of Clairvaux's works are published by Liturgical Press, Collegeville, MN. Reprinted with permission.

Five Books on Consideration: Advice to a Pope, copyright © 1976 by Cistercian Publications

On Loving God, copyright © 1974 by Cistercian Publications

On the Song of Songs I, copyright © 1971 by Cistercian Publications

On the Song of Songs II, copyright © 1976 by Cistercian Publications

On the Song of Songs III, copyright © 1979 by Cistercian Publications

On the Song of Songs IV, copyright © 1980 by Cistercian Publications

Cover design by Rosana Usselmann

Cover photo by Mary Emmanuel Alves, FSP

Published by Pauline Books & Media, 50 Saint Pauls Avenue, Boston, MA 02130-3491

Printed in the U.S.A.

www.pauline.org

Pauline Books & Media is the publishing house of the Daughters of St. Paul, an international congregation of women religious serving the Church with the communications media.

1 2 3 4 5 6 7 8 9   17 16 15 14 13

For Abbot Justin Brown, OSB

Contents

Foreword

It was Dante Alighieri, the author of the medieval masterpiece *The Divine Comedy*, who first introduced me to Saint Bernard of Clairvaux. Before Dante, I knew Saint Bernard only as a prominent figure in the Church of the twelfth century. After Dante, I came to discover why the famous Cistercian monk and reformer wielded so much influence upon an entire continent—upon popes, cardinals, and statesmen alike.

The Divine Comedy is required reading for everyone enrolled at Saint Joseph Seminary College, the college seminary run by the Benedictine monks of Saint Joseph Abbey in Saint Benedict, Louisiana, which I attended. Dante's vision of the soul's journey through *Inferno (Hell), Purgatorio*

(Purgatory), and *Paradiso (Heaven)* was exhilarating to me as a young seminarian interested in the spiritual life. Most memorable to me was the way Dante uses Beatrice, a symbol of human love and divine revelation, as his initial guide in his journey toward *Paradiso*. Unlike others who view human love and love for God as conflicting realities, Dante's world is fundamentally a sacramental one in which grace and blessing come to us in our most intimate relationships. For Dante, *Paradiso* becomes not an unexpected departure from life's previous experiences, but rather a flowering of the hidden potential of human life itself. Intimacy with others blossoms into intimacy with God.

In *Paradiso*, Saint Bernard is Dante's choice to lead him into contemplative union with God. The choice is significant. Saint Bernard is, for Dante, among the most renowned of contemplatives—one who is "absorbed in His delight."[1] Life's goal is transcendent, and Beatrice can take us only so far. We all need a Saint Bernard to guide us and keep us focused upon that which gives our lives ultimate significance—that which brings us to our true end. For Dante, this ultimate significance and true end is not discovered through intellectual assent or blind obedience, nor through achievement or heroism. Saint Bernard is chosen because Dante believes life's ultimate significance and true end is discovered only through an intimate communion with God.

It was after my course on Dante that I began reading Saint Bernard's own works. My dual interest in spirituality and Sacred Scripture led me to his crowning achievement: his eighty-six sermons titled *On the Song of Songs*. While I wasn't used to Saint Bernard's medieval, allegorical approach, I was nevertheless smitten by his rapturous, penetrating description of the soul's relationship with God. Because of Dante, I recognized that Saint Bernard wasn't just a man who had a peculiar talent as a scribe. This was a man who knew God on the most intimate terms. With clear insights into the human heart, Saint Bernard's sermons cut through the many layers of superficiality that still remained in my relationship with God and revealed to me the one thing necessary, intimacy with God. I began to realize that reading Saint Bernard was not simply a matter of reading at all: it was prayer itself—prayer on the most profound level.

Born in 1090, at the end of a century filled with monastic reforms, Saint Bernard played a leading role in one of these reforms and was largely responsible for its rapid expansion throughout Western Europe. The early Cistercians (so called after the monastery of Citeaux, the home of the reform) had one primary purpose in renewing monasticism: to simplify it. They believed this required of them a more faithful observance of the Rule of Saint Benedict. In particular, they emphasized a spirit of poverty, simplicity, and humility. Reacting to the ostentation and grandeur then found in the life and worship of other monastic orders, Cistercians sought to create an atmosphere wholly conducive to a life of contemplation. Known for their serious approach to the spiritual life, the community of monks at Citeaux caught the attention of the one who would become their monastery's greatest member.

At age twenty-four, Saint Bernard entered the monastery of Citeaux, bringing with him his brothers, an uncle, and many of his friends. Just three years later, he founded a monastery at Clairvaux and became its first abbot. In his thirty-five years as the main promoter of his Order, sixty-eight additional monasteries were founded. By his death in 1153, Cistercian monasteries comprised some 350 houses, with 164 falling more or less under his direct authority.

Such rapid expansion under Saint Bernard's tutelage evidences his charismatic personality as well as his unique influence upon the hearts of vast numbers of young men who sought a more meaningful existence. Their attraction to Saint Bernard was not based upon superficial enthusiasm. The monks' endurance, along with the tremendous expansion, attests that the men's reaction went beyond mere emotional elation.

The eighty-six sermons *On the Song of Songs* express the heart of Saint Bernard's spirituality. Written for the monks of his community, they were, nonetheless, circulated around monasteries throughout Europe with great rapidity. Using the metaphor of Bride and Bridegroom to illustrate the soul's relationship with God, Saint Bernard struck a nerve with the monks and nuns of his day. His symbols and analogy related to them the spiritual life in a way that went to the very heart of their experiences as human beings.

The spirituality of Saint Bernard may be understood, at least in part, as a response to the values of the society in which he lived. Notions of romantic love were in the air. This phenomenon (known as "courtly love" because it largely centered on courtly life) inflated the idea of human love to such an extent that love for God seemed no longer to be the true end of human life. "Falling in love" was. Whether Saint Bernard was consciously reacting against such notions is hard to say. But it seems to me that his way of interpreting the spiritual life almost exclusively in terms of intimacy with God is what sparked such a wildfire in the monastic community. Saint Bernard's compelling approach awakened people to the only relationship that truly satisfies: our relationship with God.

———— ❧ ————

It's not too difficult to make comparisons between our society and that of Saint Bernard's time. Romantic love has become one of the Western world's greatest idols. The illusion that love is mainly a feeling and that another person can fulfill all of one's needs and desires has left countless families devastated and numberless hearts shattered.

We each bring to our relationship with God the pieces of a heart that is wounded, sometimes even devastated and broken. We begin to discover, in the light of God's love, the extent to which we have cheapened ourselves by offering so indiscriminately the most intimate aspects of our hearts, minds, and bodies to things and people. In the process, we realize how much we have lost in terms of our personal integrity and dignity and how far we have fallen into a web of lies and deceit concerning what it means to be truly human.

In the midst of our yearning for wholeness and true love, God steps in and reveals to us that for which we have been searching. Reading Saint Bernard's sermons *On the Song of Songs* enabled me to discover, indeed experience, my heart's deepest desire: the reality of God's love for me.*

I identify with the cherished Bride whose Bridegroom is the Lord Jesus Christ. As I have grown in intimacy with God over the years, I have let go of many of the fears that kept me from truly sharing myself with others. My intimacy with God has also freed me of the sense of shame that once held me captive. I have learned how to become vulnerable and trusting, knowing that nothing can separate me from the love of God.

Saint Bernard's lessons on true intimacy with God have taught me how to properly love others. Instead of being caught up in the attachments that often arise from a heart divided and broken, the love of God has enabled the reservoir of love within me to flow with greater and greater freedom and purity. Ironically, the closer I come to God, the closer I am to others—even in my life as a monk.

Yet, one need not be a monk or nun to benefit from Saint Bernard's teaching on intimacy with God. All people are called to know firsthand the depth of God's love. We are all called to assume our role as the Bride of Christ and enter periodically into our Beloved's bridal chamber. The

---

* Note to the reader: In all of the selections from *On the Song of Songs*, Saint Bernard likens the human soul to a bride of Christ. In doing so, the imagery of marital intimacy is used to describe the soul's search for spiritual union with God. The unseen pursuit of a relationship with our God plays out before us as a tender love affair.

contemplative experience of being "rapt in love's bliss"[2] is not the occupation of monks and nuns alone; it is the basic vocation of every human being. Wherever we may find ourselves along life's journey, God beckons us to himself so he may lavish upon us our hearts' deepest longing.

I

An Invitation to Love

You wish me to tell you why and how God should be loved. My answer is that God himself is the reason why he is to be loved. As for how he is to be loved, there is to be no limit to that love. Is this sufficient answer? Perhaps, but only for a wise man. As I am indebted, however, to the unwise also,[1] it is customary to add something for them after saying enough for the wise. Therefore for the sake of those who are slow to grasp ideas I do not find it burdensome to treat of the same ideas more extensively if not more profoundly. Hence I insist that there are two reasons why God should be loved for his own sake: no one can be loved more righteously and no one can be loved with greater benefit. Indeed, when it is asked why God should be loved, there are two meanings possible to the question. For it can be questioned which is rather the question: whether for what merit of his or for what advantage to us is God to be loved. My answer to both questions is assuredly the same, for I can see no other reason for loving him than himself.

Faith certainly bids me love him all the more whom I regard as that much greater than I, for he not only gives me myself, he also gives me himself. . . . Why would not an artifact love its artist, if it is able to do so? Why would it not love him all it can, since it can do nothing except by his gift? In addition, the fact that man was made out of nothing, gratuitously and in this dignity, renders the debt of love clearer and proves the divine exaction more just. . . . "What shall I render to the LORD for all that he has given me?"[2] In his first work he gave me myself; in his second work he gave me himself; when he gave me himself, he gave me back myself. Given, and regiven, I owe myself twice over. What can I give God in return for himself? Even if I could give him myself a thousand times, what am I to God?[3]

God is not loved without a reward, although he should be loved without regard for one. True charity cannot be worthless, still, as "it does not seek its own advantage,"[4] it cannot be termed mercenary. Love pertains to the will, it is not a transaction; it cannot acquire or be acquired by a pact. Moving us freely, it makes us spontaneous. True love is content with itself; it has its reward, the object of its love. Whatever you seem to love because of something else, you do not really love; you really love the end pursued and not that by which it is pursued.

— Excerpts from *On Loving God* I:1, V:15; VII:17

II

Enduring Love

O Eugene,* how good it is for us to be here![1] But how much better it would be, if we could at sometime wholly follow where we have gone before in part. We have gone before in spirit, and not even our whole spirit, but only part, and too small a part. Our affections lie weighted down by this bodily mass, and cling to the mire with desires while only consideration, dry and delicate, flies before. And still with so little granted it as yet, it freely cries out, "LORD I have loved the beauty of your house and the place where your glory dwells."[2] What if the soul were totally

---

* Editor's note: Bernard is addressing Pope Eugene III.

recollected and with affections recalled from all the places they were held captive by fearing what should not be feared, loving what was unworthy, grieving vainly and more vainly rejoicing, it began to soar with total liberty, to drive on under the impulse of the spirit and to glide along in abundance of grace? And when the soul has begun to move about the illumined mansions and to examine carefully even the bosom of Abraham, and to look again upon the souls of martyrs under the altar[3] (whatever that might be[*]) dressed in their first robes[4] and patiently awaiting their second, will it not say much more insistently with the Prophet, "One thing I have asked of the LORD, this will I seek, that I may dwell in the house of the LORD all the days of my life, that I may see the will of the LORD, and visit his temple"?[5] Is not the heart of God to be seen there? Is it not shown there what is the good, the acceptable, the perfect will of God[6]: good in itself, pleasing in its effects, acceptable to those enjoying it, perfect to those who are perfect and who seek nothing beyond it? His heart of mercy lies open,[7] his thoughts of peace lie revealed,[8] the riches of his salvation,[9] the mysteries of his good will, the secrets of his kindness, which are hidden from mortals and beyond the comprehension of even the elect. This, indeed, is for the

---

[*] Editor's note: Here Bernard admits that the previous Scripture reference is too obscure for him.

good of their salvation, so they do not cease fearing before they are found suited for loving worthily.

———— ∾ ————

Holy affection makes a saint, and this affection is two-fold: holy fear of the Lord and holy love. The soul affected perfectly by these comprehends as with two arms, and embraces, binds and holds, and says, "I held him and I will not let him go." [10] Indeed, fear corresponds to height and depth; love to width and length. [11] What is so to be feared as power which you cannot resist, as wisdom from which you cannot hide? God could be feared less if he were lacking either of these. As it is, it is perfectly fitting that you fear him for he is not without an eye which sees all, nor a hand which is all-powerful. What, moreover, is so loveable as love itself, by which you love and by which you are loved? Still, it is made more loveable by its union with eternity for it dispels suspicion since it does not die. Therefore, love with perseverance and patience and you have length; widen your love to include your enemies and you possess width; also, be God-fearing and observant in everything you do and you have obtained height and depth.

— Excerpts from *Five Books on Consideration*, Book Five: 9; 30

III

The Kiss of the Lord

Today the text we are to study is the book of our own experience. You must therefore turn your attention inwards, each one must take note of his own particular awareness of the things I am about to discuss. I am attempting to discover if any of you has been privileged to say from his heart: "Let him kiss me with the kiss of his mouth."[1] Those to whom it is given to utter these words sincerely are comparatively few, but any one who has received this mystical kiss from the mouth of Christ at least once, seeks again that intimate experience, and eagerly looks for its frequent renewal. I think that nobody can grasp what it is except the one who receives it. For it is "a hidden manna," [2] and only he who eats it still hungers for more. [3] It is "a sealed fountain"[4] to which no stranger has access; only he who drinks still thirsts for more. Listen to one who has had the experience, how urgently he demands: "Be my savior again, renew my joy." But a soul like mine, burdened with sins, still subject to carnal passions, [5] devoid of any knowledge of spiritual delights, may not presume to make such a request, almost totally unacquainted as it is with the joys of the supernatural life.

You have seen the way that we must follow, the order of procedure: first, we cast ourselves at his feet, we weep before the Lord who made us, [6] deploring the evil we have done. Then we reach out for the hand that will lift us up, that will steady our trembling knees. [7] And finally, when we shall have obtained these favors through many prayers and tears, we humbly dare to raise our eyes to his mouth, so divinely beautiful, not merely to gaze upon it, but—I say it with fear and trembling—to receive its kiss. "Christ the Lord is a Spirit before our face,"[8] and he who is joined to him in a holy kiss[9] becomes through his good pleasure, one spirit with him. [10]

To you, Lord Jesus, how truly my heart has said: "My face looks to you. LORD, I do seek your face."[11] In the dawn you brought me proof of your love, in my first approach to kiss your revered feet you forgave my evil ways as I lay in the dust. With the advancement of the day you gave your servant reason to rejoice[12] when, in the kiss of the hand, you imparted the grace to live rightly. And now what remains, O good Jesus, except that suffused as I am with the fullness of your light, and while my spirit is fervent, you would graciously bestow on me the kiss of your mouth, and give me unbounded joy in your presence.[13]

— Excerpts from *On the Song of Songs*, Sermon 3:1; 5

IV

An Intimate Love

"Let him kiss me with the kiss of his mouth,"[1] she said.
Now who is this "she"? The Bride. But why Bride?
Because she is the soul thirsting for God. In order to clarify
for you the characteristics of the Bride, I shall deal briefly
with the diverse affective relationships between persons.
Fear motivates a slave's attitude to his master, gain that of
wage-earner to his employer, the learner is attentive to his
teacher, the son is respectful to his father. But the one who
asks for a kiss, she is a lover. Among all the natural endow-
ments of man love holds first place, especially when it is
directed to God, who is the source whence it comes. No
sweeter names can be found to embody that sweet

interflow of affections between the Word and the soul, than Bridegroom and Bride. Between these all things are equally shared, there are no selfish reservations, nothing that causes division. They share the same inheritance, the same table, the same home, the same marriage-bed, they are flesh of each other's flesh. "This is why a man leaves his father and mother and joins himself to his wife, and they become one body."[2] The Bride for her part is bidden to "forget her nation and her ancestral home," so that the Bridegroom may fall in love with her beauty.[3] Therefore if a love relationship is the special and outstanding characteristic of the Bride and Groom, it is not unfitting to call the soul that loves God a Bride. Now one who asks for a kiss is in love. It is not for liberty that she asks, nor for an award, not for an inheritance nor even knowledge, but for a kiss. It is obviously the request of a Bride who is chaste, who breathes forth a love that is holy, a love whose ardor she cannot entirely disguise. For note how abruptly she bursts into speech. About to ask a great favor from a great personage, she does not resort, as others do, to the arts of seduction, she makes no devious or fawning solicitations for the prize that she covets. There is no preamble, no attempt to conciliate favor. No, but with a spontaneous outburst from the abundance of her heart,[4] direct even to the point of boldness, she says: "Let him kiss me with the kiss of his mouth."

Does not this seem to you to indicate that she wished to say: "Whom have I in heaven but you? And there is nothing upon earth that I desire besides you."[5]

Her love is surely chaste when it seeks the person whom she loves, and not some other thing of his. It is a holy love, the impulse of an upright spirit rather than a carnal desire. And it is an ardent love, blinded by its own excess to the majesty of the beloved. For what are the facts? He is the one at whose glance the earth trembles,[6] and does she demand that he give her a kiss? Can she be possibly drunk? Absolutely drunk! And the reason? It seems most probable that when she uttered those passionate words she had just come out from the cellar of wine;[7] afterward she boasts of having been there. David in his turn cried out to God concerning people such as the Bride: "They shall be inebriated with the plenty of your house; and you will make them drink of the torrent of your pleasure."[8] How great this power of love: what great confidence and freedom of spirit! What is more manifest than that fear is driven out by perfect love![9]

— Excerpt from *On the Song of Songs*, Sermon 7:2–3

V

The Spirit of Love

You too, if you would make prudent progress in your studies of the mysteries of the faith, would do well to remember the Wise Man's advice: "Do not try to understand things that are too difficult for you, or try to discover what is beyond your powers."[1] These are occasions when you must walk by the Spirit[2] and not according to your personal opinions, for the Spirit teaches not by sharpening curiosity but by inspiring charity. And hence the Bride, when seeking him whom her heart loves,[3] quite properly does not put her trust in mere human prudence, nor yield to the inane conceits of human curiosity. She asks rather for a kiss, that is, she calls upon the Holy Spirit by whom she is simultaneously awarded with the choice repast of knowledge and the seasoning of grace. How true it is that the knowledge imparted in the kiss is lovingly received, since the kiss is love's own token. But knowledge which leads to self-importance,[4] since it is devoid of love, cannot be the fruit of the kiss. Even those who have a zeal for God, but not according to knowledge,[5] may not for any reason lay claim to that kiss. For the favor of the kiss bears with it a twofold gift, the light of knowledge and the fervor of devotion. He is in truth the Spirit of wisdom and insight, who, like the bee carrying its burden of wax and honey, is fully equipped with the power both of kindling the light of knowledge and infusing the delicious nurture of grace. Two kinds of people therefore may not consider themselves to have been gifted with the kiss, those who know the truth without loving it, and those who love it without understanding it; from which we conclude that this kiss leaves room neither for ignorance nor for lukewarmness.

So therefore, let the Bride about to receive the twofold grace of this most holy kiss set her two lips in readiness, her reason for the gift of insight, her will for that of wisdom, so that overflowing with joy in the fullness of this kiss, she may be privileged to hear the words: "Your lips are moist with grace, for God has blessed you forever."[6]

Thus the Father, when he kisses the Son, pours into him the plenitude of the mysteries of his divine being, breathing forth love's deep delight, as symbolized in the words of the psalm: "Day to day pours forth speech."[7] As has already been stated, no creature whatsoever has been privileged to comprehend the secret of this eternal, blessed, and unique embrace; the Holy Spirit alone is the sole witness and confidant of their mutual knowledge and love. For who could ever know the mind of the Lord, or who could be his counselor?[8]

— Excerpt from *On the Song of Songs,* Sermon 8:6

VI

Rest in God

"I cannot rest," she said, "unless he kisses me with the kiss of his mouth."[1] I thank him for the kiss of the feet, I thank him too for the kiss of the hand; but if he has genuine regard for me, let him kiss me with the kiss of his mouth. There is no question of ingratitude on my part, it is simply that I am in love. The favors I have received are far above what I deserve, but they are less than what I long for. It is desire that drives me on, not reason. Please do not accuse me of presumption if I yield to this impulse of love. My shame indeed rebukes me, but love is stronger than all. I am well aware that he is a king who loves justice;[2] but headlong love does not wait for judgment, is not chastened by advice, not shackled by shame nor subdued by reason. I ask, I crave, I implore; let him kiss me with the kiss of his mouth. Don't you see that by his grace I have been for many years now careful to lead a chaste and sober life,[3] I concentrate on spiritual studies, resist vices, pray often; I am watchful against temptations, I recount all my years in the bitterness of my soul.[4] As far as I can judge I have lived among the brethren without quarrel.[5] I have been submissive to authority,[6] responding to the beck and call of my superior. I do not covet goods not mine; rather do I put both myself and my goods at the service of others. With sweat on my brow I eat my bread.[7] Yet in all these practices there is evidence only of my fidelity, nothing of enjoyment. What can I be but, in the words of the Prophet, another Ephraim, a well-trained heifer that loves to tread the threshing floor?[8] On top of that the Gospel says that he who does no more than his duty is looked on as a useless servant.[9] I obey the commandments, to the best of my ability I hope, but in doing so 'my soul thirsts like a parched land.'[10] If therefore he is to find my holocaust acceptable,[11] let him kiss me, I entreat, with the kiss of his mouth."

Many of you too, as I recall, are accustomed to complain to me in our private conversations about a similar languor and dryness of soul, an ineptitude and dullness of mind devoid of the power to penetrate the profound and subtle truths of God; devoid too, entirely or for the most part, of the sweetness of the spirit. What of these, except that they yearn to be kissed? That they yearn is indeed evident, their very mouths are open to inhale the spirit of wisdom and insight:[12] insight that they may attain to what they long for, wisdom in order to savor what the mind apprehends. I think that a motive such as this must have inspired the holy Prophet's prayer when he said: "My soul will feast most richly, on my lips a song of joy and in my mouth, praise."[13] The kiss was surely what he sought for, that kiss at whose touch the lips are so bedewed with the richness of spiritual grace, that only the Prophet's words again, spoken in another context, can fathom the effect: "My mouth is full of your praises, that I might sing of your glory, of your splendor all day long."[14] No sooner had he tasted than he burst forth: "LORD how great your goodness, reserved for those who fear you!"[15]

— Excerpt from *On the Song of Songs*, Sermon 9:2–3

VII

The Touch of the Lord

It adds strength to my confidence to think that the great Prophet, mighty in work and word,[1] came down from heaven's high mountain to visit me who am but dust and ashes,[2] pitying me in my spiritual death, stretching himself upon me as I lay prone, diminishing his stature to be equal to my littleness, sharing with my blindness the light of his own eyes, freeing my dumbness with the kiss of his mouth, and bracing my weak hands with the touch of his own. To linger amid these truths is my delight; my heart is enlarged, my whole inward being is enriched,[3] my very bones vibrate with praise.[4] He performed this work once for the human race as a whole, but daily each one of us may experience it in ourselves, when the light of understanding floods our heart, when helpful words grace our speech, when good deeds flow from our hands. By his grace we can think what is true, we can express it to advantage, we can live it with efficacy. Here you are provided with a durable three-ply cord[5] for drawing souls out of the devil's prison, and towing them after you into the kingdom of heaven; if you think rightly, if you speak worthily, and if you confirm what you say by your life. Covering my eyes with his own he adorned my interior faculties with the twin lights of faith and understanding. Joining his mouth to this dead mouth of mine, he gave the kiss of peace, for while we were yet sinners and dead to righteousness, he reconciled us to God.[6] Setting his mouth to mine he breathed into it a second time the breath of life,[7] but this time a holier life; for at first he created me a living being, then re-made me a life-giving spirit.[8] As he placed his hands on mine I was imbued with the power of doing good,[9] with the grace of obedience. He certainly showed how strong his hands can be,[10] that he might train my hands for war and my fingers for battle.[11]

O Wisdom, sweetly powerful and powerfully sweet, with what skill of healing in wine and oil do you restore my soul's health. Powerfully for me and sweet to me. You deploy your strength from one end of the earth to the other, ordering all things sweetly,[12] driving off all hostile powers and cherishing the weak. Heal me, Lord, and I shall really be healed,[13] I shall sing praise to your name[14] and cry out: "Your name is oil poured out.[15] Not wine poured out—for I do not wish to be put on trial[16]—but oil, for you crown me with love and tenderness.[17] Oil by all means, for since it floats above all other liquids with which it mixes, it clearly designates a name that is above all names.[18] O Name utterly dear, utterly sweet! O Name renowned, predestined, sublime and exalted above all for ever.[19] This is truly the oil that makes a man's face shine,[20] that anoints the head of the man who fasts, causing him to ignore the oil of sinners.[21] This is the new Name which the mouth of the LORD has conferred,[22] the Name given by the angel before he was conceived in the womb."[23] Not the Jews only, but all who call on that name will be saved,[24] for it has been poured out without limit. This was the Father's gift to the Son, the Church's Bridegroom, our Lord, Jesus Christ, who is blessed for ever.[25] Amen.

— Excerpts from *On the Song of Songs,* Sermon 16:2; 15

VIII

The Wonder of God's Love

How wonderful your love for me, my God, my love! How wonderful your love for me, everywhere mindful of me, everywhere eager for the welfare of one who is needy and poor, protecting him both from the arrogance of men and from the might of evil spirits. Both in heaven and on earth, O LORD, you accuse my accusers, you attack my attackers;[1] everywhere you bring help, always you are close to my right hand lest I be disturbed.[2] "I will sing to the LORD as long as I live, I will sing praise to my God while I have being."[3] How great are his powers, what wonders has he not done![4] The first and greatest of his achievements is that revealed to me by one initiated to his mysteries, the Virgin Mary: "He has pulled down princes from their thrones and exalted the lowly. The hungry he has filled with good things, the rich sent away empty."[5] The second you have heard of too, it is like the first: "That those without sight may see, and those with sight turn blind."[6] These two judgments are the poor man's consolation, they enable him to say: "Remembering your rulings in the past, LORD, I take comfort."[7]

Let us return now to ourselves, let us examine our paths;[8] and in order to accomplish this in truth, let us invoke the Spirit of truth,[9] let us call to him from the deep into which he has led us, because he leads us on the way by which we discover ourselves, and without him we can do nothing.[10] Nor should we be afraid that he will disdain to come down to us, for the contrary is true: he is displeased if we attempt even the least thing without him. For he is not one "who passes and does not return,"[11] he leads us on from brightness to brightness because he is the Spirit of the Lord.[12] Sometimes he fills us with rapture by communication of his light, sometimes he adapts himself to our weakness and sends beams of light into the dark about us.[13] But whether we are raised above ourselves or left with ourselves, let us stay always in the light, always walk as children of the light.[14] And now that we have passed through the shadow-land of allegories, it is time to explore the great plains of moral truths.[15] Our faith has been strengthened, let our lives reveal its influence; our intellects have been enlightened, let them prescribe the right behavior. For they have sound sense who do this,[16] if they direct their actions and understanding toward the praise and glory of our Lord Jesus Christ,[17] who is blessed for ever.[18]

— Excerpt from *On the Song of Songs,* Sermon 17:7–8

IX

The Right Kind of Love

I would like to begin with a word from Saint Paul: "If anyone does not love the Lord Jesus, let him be anathema."[1] Truly, I ought to love the one through whom I have my being, my life, my understanding. If I am ungrateful, I am unworthy too. Lord Jesus, whoever refuses to live for you is clearly worthy of death, and is in fact dead already. Whoever does not know you is a fool. And whoever wants to become something without you, without doubt that man is considered nothing and is just that. For what is man, unless you take notice of him?[2] You have made all things for yourself, O God, and whoever wants to live for himself and not for you, in all that he does, is nothing.

"Fear God, and keep his commandments," it is said, "for this is the whole duty of man."[3] So if this is all, without this, man is nothing. Turn toward yourself, O God, this little that you have granted me to be; take from this miserable life, I beg you, the years that remain.[4] In place of all that I lost in my evil way of living, O God, do not refuse a humble and penitent heart.[5] My days have lengthened like a shadow and passed without fruit.[6] I cannot bring them back, but let it please you at least if I offer them to you in the bitterness of my soul.[7] As for wisdom—my every desire and intention is before you[8]—if there were any in me, I would keep it for you. But, God, you know my stupidity,[9] unless perhaps it is wisdom for me to recognize it, and even this is your gift. Grant me more; not that I am ungrateful for this small gift, but that I am eager for what is lacking. For all these things, and as much as I am able, I love you.

But there is something else that moves me, arouses and enflames me even more. Good Jesus, the chalice you drank, the price of our redemption, makes me love you more than all the rest. This alone would be enough to claim our love. This, I say, is what wins our love so sweetly, justly demands it, firmly binds it, deeply affects it. Our Savior had to toil so hard in this, in fact in making the whole world the Creator did not labor so much. Then he spoke and they were made; he commanded and they were created.[10] But in saving us he had to endure men who contradicted his words, criticized his actions, ridiculed his suffering, and mocked his death. See how much he loved us.

———— ❧ ————

Christian, learn from Christ how you ought to love Christ. Learn a love that is tender, wise, strong; love with tenderness, not passion, wisdom, not foolishness, and strength, lest you become weary and turn away from the love of the Lord. Do not let the glory of the world or the pleasure of the flesh lead you astray; the wisdom of Christ should become sweeter to you than these. The light of Christ should shine so much for you that the spirit of lies and deceit will not seduce you. Finally, Christ as the strength of God should support you so that you may not be worn down by difficulties.[11] Let love enkindle your zeal, let knowledge inform it, let constancy strengthen it. Keep it fervent, discreet, courageous. See it is not tepid, or temerarious, or timid. See for yourself if those three commands are not prescribed in the law when God says: "You shall love the Lord your God with your whole heart, your whole soul and your whole strength."[12] It seems to me, if no more suitable meaning for this triple distinction comes to mind, that the love of the heart relates to a certain warmth of affection, the love of the soul to energy or judgment or reason, and the love of strength can refer to constancy and vigor of spirit. So love the Lord your God with the full and deep affection of your heart, love him with your mind wholly awake and discreet, love him with all your strength, so much so that you would not even fear to die for love of him. As it is written: "For love is strong as death, jealousy is bitter as hell." [13] Your affection for your Lord Jesus should be both tender and intimate, to oppose the sweet entice-ments of sensual life. Sweetness conquers sweetness as one nail drives out another. No less than this keep him as a strong light for your mind and a guide for your intellect, not only to avoid the deceits of heresy and to preserve the purity of your faith from their seductions, but also that you might carefully avoid an indiscreet and excessive vehe-mence in your conversation. Let your love be strong and constant, neither yielding to fear nor cowering at hard work. Let us love affectionately, discreetly, intensely. We know that the love of the heart, which we have said is affectionate, is sweet indeed, but liable to be led astray if it lacks the love of the soul. And the love of the soul is wise indeed, but fragile without that love which is called love of strength.

— Excerpts from *On the Song of Songs,* Sermon 20:1–2; 4

X

In the Room of the King

B ut there is a place where God is seen in tranquil rest, where he is neither Judge nor Teacher but Bridegroom. To me—for I do not speak for others—this is truly the bedroom to which I have sometimes gained happy entrance. Alas! How rare the time, and how short the stay! There one clearly realizes that "the LORD's love for those who fear him lasts forever and forever."[1] It is there that one may happily say: "I am a friend to all who fear you and observe your precepts."[2] God's purpose stands fast, the peace he has planned for those who fear him is without recall. Overlooking their faults and rewarding their good deeds, with a divine deftness he turns to their benefit not only the good they do but even the evil.[3] He alone is happy "whom the LORD accuses of no guilt."[4] There is no one without sin, not even one. "For all have sinned and forfeited God's glory."[5] But "could anyone accuse those that God has chosen?"[6] I ask no further pledge of righteousness if he is on my side whom alone I have offended.[7] If he decrees that a sin is not to be imputed to me, it is as if it never existed. Inability to sin constitutes God's righteousness; God's forgiveness constitutes man's. When I grasped this I understood the truth of the words: "We know that anyone who has been begotten by God does not sin, because a heavenly birth protects him."[8] Heavenly birth is eternal predestination, by which God loved his chosen ones and endowed them with spiritual blessings in his beloved Son before the world was made.[9] Thus appearing before him in his holy place,[10] they would see his power and his glory, and become sharers in the inheritance of the Son to whose image they were to be conformed.[11] I think of such as these as if they had never sinned, because the sins they committed in time do not appear in eternity, for the love of the Father covers a multitude of sins.[12] "Happy is the man whose fault is forgiven, whose sin is blotted out."[13] When I say these words I am suddenly inspired with so great a confidence, filled with such joy, that it surpasses the fear I experienced in the place of horror. . . . [14] Would that this moment lasted! Again and again visit me, LORD, in your saving mission; let me see the goodness of your chosen, let me rejoice in the joy of your nation. [15]

O place so truly quiet, so aptly called a bedroom, where God is not encountered in angry guise nor distracted as it were by cares, but where his will is proved good and desirable and perfect. [16] This is a vision that charms rather than terrifies; that does not arouse an inquisitive restlessness, but restrains it; that calms rather than wearies the senses. Here one may indeed be at rest. The God of peace pacifies all things, and to gaze on this stillness is to find repose. It is to catch sight of the King who, when the crowds have gone after the day-long hearing of cases in his law-courts, lays aside the burden of responsibility, goes at night to his place, and enters his bedroom with a few companions whom he welcomes to the intimacy of his private suite. He is all the more secure the more secluded his place of rest, all the more at ease when his placid gaze sees about him none but well-loved friends. If it should ever happen to one of you to be enraptured and hidden away in this secret place, this sanctuary of God, safe from the call and concern of the greedy senses, from the pangs of care, the guilt of sin, and the obsessive fancies of the imagination so much more difficult to hold at bay—such a man, when he returns to us again, may well boast and tell us: "The King has brought me into his bedroom." [17]

— Excerpt from *On the Song of Songs*, Sermon 23:15

XI

The Capacity for God

What a capacity this soul has, how privileged its merits, that it is found worthy not only to receive the divine presence, but to be able to make sufficient room! What can I say of her who can provide avenues spacious enough for the God of majesty to walk in! She certainly cannot afford to be entangled in law-suits nor by worldly cares; she cannot be enslaved by gluttony and sensual pleasures, by the lust of the eyes, the ambition to rule, or by pride in the possession of power. If she is to become heaven, the dwelling-place of God, it is first of all essential that she be empty of all these defects. Otherwise how could she be still enough to know that he is God?[1] Nor may she yield in the least to hatred or envy or bitterness, "because wisdom will not enter a deceitful soul."[2] The soul must grow and expand, that it may be roomy enough for God. Its width is its love, if we accept what the Apostle says: "Widen your hearts in love."[3] The soul, being a spirit, does not admit of material expansion, but grace confers gifts on it that nature is not equipped to bestow. Its growth and expansion must be understood in a spiritual sense; it is its virtue that increases, not its substance. Even its glory is increased. And finally it grows and advances toward "mature manhood, to the measure of the stature of the fullness of Christ."[4] Eventually it becomes "a holy temple in the Lord."[5] The capacity of any man's soul is judged by the amount of love he possesses; hence he who loves much is great, he who loves a little is small, he who has no love is nothing, as Paul said: "If I have not love, I am nothing."[6] But if he begins to acquire some love however, if he tries at least to love those who love him,[7] and salutes the brethren and others who salute him,[8] I may no longer describe him as nothing because some love must be present in the give and take of social life.[9] In the words of the Lord, however, what more is he doing than others.[10] When I discover a love as mediocre as this, I cannot call such a man noble or great: he is obviously narrow-minded and mean.

But if his love expands and continues to advance till it outgrows these narrow, servile confines, and finds itself in the open ranges where love is freely given in full liberty of spirit; when from the generous bounty of his goodwill he strives to reach out to all his neighbors, loving each of them as himself,[11] surely one may no longer query, "What more are you doing than others?" Indeed he has made himself vast. His heart is filled with a love that embraces everybody, even those to whom it is not tied by the inseparable bonds of family relationship; a love that is not allured by any hope of personal gain, that possesses nothing it is obliged to restore, that bears no burden of debt whatever, apart from that one of which it is said: "Owe no one anything, except to love one another."[12] Progressing further still, you may endeavor to take the kingdom of love by force,[13] until by this holy warfare you succeed in possessing it even to its farthest bounds. Instead of shutting off your affections from your enemies,[14] you will do good to those who hate you, you will pray for those who persecute and slander you,[15] you will strive to be peaceful even with those who hate peace.[16] Then the width, height, and beauty of your soul will be the width, height, and beauty of heaven itself, and you will realize how true it is that he has "stretched out the heavens like a curtain."[17] In this heaven whose width, height, and beauty compel our admiration, he who is supreme and immense and glorious is not only pleased to dwell, but to wander far and wide on its pathways.

— Excerpt from *On the Song of Songs*, Sermon 27:10–11

XII

A Face-to-Face Encounter

One who is so disposed and so beloved will by no means be content either with that manifestation of the Bridegroom given to the many in the world of creatures,[1] or to the few in visions and dreams. By a special privilege she wants to welcome him down from heaven into her inmost heart, into her deepest love; she wants to have the one she desires present to her not in bodily form but by inward infusion, not by appearing externally but by laying hold of her within. It is beyond question that the vision is all the more delightful the more inward it is, and not external. It is the Word, who penetrates without sound; who is effective though not pronounced, who wins the affections without striking on the ears. His face, though without form, is the source of form, it does not dazzle the eyes of the body but gladdens the watchful heart; its pleasure is in the gift of love and not in the color of the lover.

Not yet have I come round to saying that he has appeared as he is, although in this inward vision he does not reveal himself as altogether different from what he is. Neither does he make his presence continuously felt, not even to his most ardent lovers, nor in the same way to all. For the various desires of the soul it is essential that the taste of God's presence be varied too, and that the infused flavor of divine delight should titillate in manifold ways the palate of the soul that seeks him. You must already have noticed how often he changes his countenance in the course of this love-song, how he delights in transforming himself from one charming guise to another in the beloved's presence: at one moment like a bashful Bridegroom maneuvering for the hidden embraces of his holy lover, for the bliss of her kisses; at another coming along like a physician with oil and ointments, because weak and tender souls still need remedies and medicines of this kind, which is why they are rather daintily described as maidens. Should anybody find fault with this, let him be told that "it is not the healthy who need the doctor, but the sick."[2] Sometimes, too, he joins up as a traveler with the Bride and the maidens who accompany her on the road,

46

and lightens the hardships of the journey for the whole company by his fascinating conversation, so that when he has parted from them they ask: "Did not our hearts burn within us as he talked to us on the road?"[3] A silver-tongued companion who, by the spell of his words and manners, persuades everyone, as if in a sweet-smelling cloud arising from the ointments, to follow him. Hence they say: "We will run after you in the odor of your ointments."[4] At another time he comes to meet them as a wealthy father of a family "with bread enough and to spare"[5] in his house; or again like a magnificent and powerful king, giving courage to his timid and poverty-stricken Bride, stirring up her desire by showing her the ornaments of his glory, the riches of his wine-presses and storehouse, the produce of his gardens and fields, and finally introducing her into his private apartments.[6] For "her husband's heart has confidence in her,"[7] and among all his possessions there is nothing that he thinks should be hidden from her whom he redeemed from indigence, whose fidelity he has proved, whose attractiveness wins his embraces. And so he never ceases, in one way or another, to reveal himself to the inward eye of those who seek him, thus fulfilling the promise that he made: "Be assured I am with you always, to the end of time."[8]

— Excerpt from *On the Song of Songs,* Sermon 31:6–7

XIII

Athirst for God

If then, any of us, like the holy Prophet, finds that it is good to cling close to God,[1] and—that I may make my meaning more clear—if any of us is so filled with desire[2] that he wants to depart and to be with Christ,[3] with a desire that is intense, a thirst ever burning, an application that never flags, he will certainly meet the Word in the guise of a Bridegroom on whatever day he comes.[4] At such an hour he will find himself locked in the arms of Wisdom; he will experience how sweet divine love is as it flows into his heart. His heart's desire will be given to him,[5] even while still a pilgrim on earth,[6] though not in its fullness and only for a time, a short time. For when after vigils and prayers and a great shower of tears he who was sought presents himself, suddenly he is gone again, just when we think we hold him fast. But he will present himself anew to the soul that pursues him with tears, for suddenly a second time he flees from between our hands. And if the fervent soul persists with prayers and tears, he will return each time and not defraud him of his express desire,[7] but only to disappear soon again and not to return unless he is sought for with all one's heart. And so, even in this body we can often enjoy the happiness of the Bridegroom's presence, but it is a happiness that is never complete because the joy of the visit is followed by the pain at his departure. The beloved has no choice but to endure this state until the hour when she lays down the body's weary weight, and raised aloft on the wings of desire, freely traverses the meadows of contemplation, and in spirit follows the One she loves without restraint wherever he goes.[8]

Nevertheless, he will not reveal himself in this way to every person, even momentarily, but only to the one who is proved to be a worthy Bride by intense devotion, vehement desire and the sweetest affection. And the Word who comes to visit will be clothed in beauty,[9] in every aspect a Bridegroom.

But the person who has not yet been raised to this state, who smarts at the remembrance of past deeds and says to God in bitterness of soul, "Do not condemn me,"[10] or who may still be caught up in the snare of his own evil propensities, still perilously tempted,[11] this person needs a physician, not a Bridegroom; hence kisses and embraces are not for him, but only oil and ointments, remedies for his wounds. Is not this how we too often feel? Is not this our experience at prayer, we who are tempted daily by our passions and filled with remorse for our past sins? O good Jesus, from what great bitterness have you not freed me by your coming, time after time? When distress has made me weep, when untold sobs and groans have shaken me, have you not anointed my wounded conscience with the ointment of your mercy and poured in the oil of gladness?[12] How often has not prayer raised me from the brink of despair and made me feel happy in the hope of pardon? All who have had these experiences know well that the Lord Jesus is a physician indeed, "who heals the broken-hearted and binds up their wounds."[13] And those who cannot lay claim to experience must for that very reason put their trust in him when he says: "The Spirit of the LORD has anointed me, he has sent me to bring good news to the humble, to bind up the broken-hearted."[14] And if they should still be in doubt, let them draw near and put it to the test and so learn by inward experience what this means: "I desire mercy and not sacrifice."[15]

— Excerpt from *On the Song of Songs,* Sermon 32:2–3

XIV

Alone with God

O holy soul, remain alone, so that you might keep yourself for him alone whom you have chosen for yourself out of all that exist. Avoid going abroad, avoid even the members of your household; withdraw from friends and those you love, not excepting the man who provides for your needs. Can you not see how shy your Love is, that he will never come to you when others are present? Therefore you must withdraw mentally rather than physically, in your intention, in your devotion, in your spirit. For Christ the Lord is a spirit before your face,[1] and he demands solitude of the spirit more than of the body, although physical withdrawal can be of benefit when the opportunity offers, especially in time of prayer. To do this is to follow the advice and example of the Bridegroom, that when you want to pray you should go into your room, shut the door, and then pray.[2] And what he said he did. He spent nights alone in prayer,[3] not merely hiding from the crowds[4] but even from his disciples and familiar friends. He did indeed take three of his friends with him when the hour of his death was approaching;[5] but the urge to pray drew him apart even from them. You too must act like this[6] when you wish to pray.

Apart from that the only solitude prescribed for you is that of the mind and spirit. You enjoy this solitude if you refuse to share in the common gossip, if you shun involvement in the problems of the hour and set no store by the fancies that attract the masses, if you reject what everybody covets, avoid disputes, make light of losses, and pay no heed to injuries.[7] Otherwise you are not alone even when alone. Do you not see that you can be alone when in company and in company when alone? However great the crowds that surround you, you can enjoy the benefits of solitude if you refrain from curiosity about other people's conduct and shun rash judgment. Even if you should see your neighbor doing what is wrong, refuse to pass judgment on him, excuse him instead. Excuse his intention even if you cannot excuse the act, which may be the fruit of ignorance or surprise or chance. Even if you are so certain that to dissemble is impossible, you must still endeavor to convince yourself by saying: "It was an over-whelming temptation; what should become of me if it attacked me with the same force?" Remember too that all this time I have been speaking to the Bride, not to the friend of the Bridegroom, who has another reason for keeping careful watch to prevent his charge from sinning, to examine if sin has been committed, and to administer correction when it has. The Bride is free from this kind of obligation, she lives alone for the love of him who is her Bridegroom and Lord, who is God blessed for ever. Amen.[8]

— Excerpt from *On the Song of Songs,* Sermon 40:4–5

XV

A Loving Affirmation

"Behold, how beautiful you are, my dearest," he said, "how beautiful."[1] "Behold," is an expression of his admiration; the rest, his praise. And how worthy of admiration she is, in whom not the loss but the preservation of holiness fostered humility. Rightly too is this beauty praised twice over, since she lacked neither of the two sources of beauty. This is a rare bird on earth,[2] where neither innocence is lost nor humility excluded by innocence. Consequently she who retained both is truly blessed. The proof is that though conscious of no fault[3] she did not reject the connection. We, when we sin gravely, can scarcely tolerate reproof; she on the contrary listens with equanimity to bitter reprimands,[4] and does not sin. If she did long to see her Bridegroom's glory, what harm in that? It is a praiseworthy desire. And yet when reproved she repented and said: "My beloved is to me a little bundle of myrrh that lies between my breasts."[5] As much as to say: It is enough for me; I desire to know nothing any longer except Jesus and him crucified.[6] What great humility! Though actually innocent she adopts the attitude of the penitent, and though conscious of nothing for which to repent, she still had the will to repent. But why then, you ask, was she reprimanded if she did nothing wrong? But listen now to the plan and the prudence of the Bridegroom. In the same way that Abraham's obedience was put to the test long ago, so now the humility of the Bride. And just as Abraham, when he carried out the command was told: "Now I know that you fear God";[7] so she is equivalently told: Now I know that you are humble. What he actually says is: "Behold, how beautiful you are."

When the Word therefore tells the soul, "You are beautiful," and calls it friend,[8] he infuses into it the power to love, and to know it is loved in return. And when the soul addresses him as beloved and praises his beauty, she is filled with admiration for his goodness and attributes to him without subterfuge or deceit the grace by which she loves and is loved. The Bridegroom's beauty is his love of the Bride, all the greater in that it existed before hers. Realizing then that he was her lover before he was her beloved, she cries out with strength and ardor that she must love him with her whole heart and with words expressing deepest affection. The speech of the Word is an infusion of grace, the soul's response is wonder and thanksgiving. The more she feels surpassed in her loving the more she gives in love; and her wonder grows when he still exceeds her. Hence, not satisfied to tell him once that he is beautiful, she repeats the word, to signify by that repetition the pre-eminence of his beauty.

— Excerpts from *On the Song of Songs,* Sermon 45:3, 8

XVI

The Embrace of God

"Prop me up with flowers, encompass me with apples, because I languish with love."[1] When that which is loved is at hand, love thrives; when absent it languishes. This is simply the weariness of impatient desire by which the mind of the ardent lover is necessarily afflicted when the loved one is absent; wholly absorbed in expectation, she reckons even any haste to be slow. And therefore she asks for an assortment of the fruits of good works made fragrant by faith in which she may rest while the Bridegroom tarries.[2] I am telling you of what comes within my own experience. Whenever I discover that any of you have benefited from my admonitions, then I confess that I never regret preferring the preparation of my sermon to my personal leisure and quietude. When, for example, after a sermon the angry man is found to have become gentle, the proud man humble, the timid man brave; or when someone who is gentle, humble, and brave has made progress in these gifts and admits that he is better than before, when those who perchance were lukewarm and tired of spiritual studies, benumbed and sleepy, and seen to grow eager and vigilant again through the burning words of the Lord; when those who, deserting the fountain of wisdom, have dug for themselves wells of self-will that cannot hold water[3] and, afflicted in consequence by every command, have been murmuring in dryness of heart because they possessed no moisture and devotion[4]—when these, I repeat, are shown through the dew of the Word and the abundant rain that God provides for those who are his,[5] to prosper again in works of obedience, to be prompt and devoted in all things, there is no reason for sorrow to invade the mind because it is interrupted in its pursuit of sweet contemplation, for I shall be surrounded by these flowers and fruits of love. Where the fruits of your progress grow in profusion about me I patiently accept being torn away from the unfruitful embraces of Rachel.* The

---

* Editor's note: This seems to be a reference to Gen 29:31.

interruption of my leisure in order to prepare a sermon will not trouble me in the least when I shall see my seed germinating in you[6] and an increase in the growth of the harvest of your righteousness.[7] For love, which does not seek what is its own,[8] has long since easily convinced me not to prefer my own cherished desires to your gain. To pray, to read, to write, to meditate, or any other gains that may result from the study of spiritual things: these I consider loss because of you.[9]

Then come the words: "His left arm under my head, his right arm will embrace me."[10] . . . It is clear that the Bridegroom has returned for the purpose of comforting the distressed Bride by his presence. How could she who had been prostrated by his absence not grow strong in his presence? Therefore he does not tolerate the affliction of his beloved. He is at her side, nor can he delay when summoned by desires so great. And because he found that during his absence she had been faithful in good works and eager for gain, in that she had ordered that flowers and fruits be given to her, of course, he returns this time with an even richer reward of grace. As she lies back he cushions her head on one of his arms, embracing her with the other, to cherish her at his bosom. Happy the soul who reclines on the breast of Christ,[11] and rests between the arms of the Word!

— Excerpts from *On the Song of Songs,* Sermon 51:3, 5

XVII

Aflame with Holy Love

What is this that she says: "He is mine and I am his"?[1] We do not know what she says, because we do not know what she feels.[2] O holy soul, what is your beloved to you? What are you to him? What is this intimate relationship, this pledge given and received? He is yours, you in turn are his. But are you to him what he is to you, or is there some difference? If you will, speak to us, to our understanding, tell us clearly what you feel.[3] How long will you keep us in expectation? Is your secret to be for you alone?[4] It is thus: it is the *affectus*,* not the intellect,

---

* Editor's note: the "heart," the affection, the passions.

which has spoken, and it is not for the intellect to grasp. What then is the reason for these words? There is none, except that the Bride is transported with delight and enraptured by the long-awaited words of the Bridegroom, and when words ceased she could neither keep silence nor yet express what she felt. Nor did she speak thus to express her feelings but merely to break her silence. "Out of the fullness of the heart the mouth speaks,"[5] but not in the same measure. The *affectus* have their own language, in which they disclose themselves even against their will. Fear has its trembling, grief its anguished groans, love its cries of delight. Are the lamentations of mourners, the sobs of those who grieve, the sighs of those in pain, the sudden frenzied screams of those in fear, the yawns of the replete— are these the result of habit? Do they constitute a reasoned discourse, a deliberate utterance, a premeditated speech? Most certainly such expressions of feeling are not produced by the processes of the mind, but by spontaneous impulses. So a strong and burning love, particularly the love of God, does not stop to consider the order, the grammar, the flow, or the number of the words it employs, when it cannot contain itself, providing it senses that it suffers no loss thereby. Sometimes it needs no words, no expression at all, being content with aspirations alone. Thus it is that the Bride, aflame with holy love, doubtless

XVIII

Confidence in the Love of God

Consider how great is the grace of intimacy which results from this encounter of the soul and the Word, and how great the confidence which follows this intimacy! I think such a soul need not fear to say, "my beloved is mine";[1] for she perceives that she loves, and loves ardently, and has no doubt that she is loved ardently in return. Then by virtue of the single-minded devotion of the watchfulness, the care and attention, the diligence and zeal with which she has ceaselessly and ardently studied to please God,[2] she recognizes these attributes in him also, with certainty and peace, recalling his promise "with what measure you measure it shall be measured out to you in return."[3]

Yet the Bride is prudent and careful to take as her share only thankfulness for grace received, for she knows that the initiative lies with the Bridegroom. Thus it is that she mentions his part first: "My beloved is mine and I am his."[4] She knows then without any doubt, from the attributes which have their origin in God, that she who loves is herself loved. And so it is: the love of God gives birth to the love of the soul for God, and his surpassing affection fills the soul with affection, and his concern evokes concern. For when the soul can once perceive the glory of God without a veil,[5] it is compelled by some affinity of nature to be conformed to it, and be transformed to its very image. So God must appear to you as you have appeared to God; "with the holy he will be holy, and with an innocent man he will be innocent."[6] Why not also loving with the loving, eager with the eager, and concerned with those who are concerned?

Lastly, he says, "I love those who love me and they who seek me early shall find me."[7] See how he assures you of his love, if you love him, and of his concern for you, if he sees you concerned for him. Do you keep watch? He keeps watch also. If you rise at night before the time of vigil[8] and hasten to anticipate the morning watch,[9] you will find him there. He will always be waiting for you. You would be very rash if you claimed to love him first or love him more; his love is greater, and it preceded yours. If the soul knows this—or because she knows it—is it any wonder that this soul, this Bride, boasts that that great majesty cares for her alone as though he had no others to care for, and she sets aside all her cares and devotes herself to him alone with all her heart. I must bring this sermon to an end, but I will say one thing to the spiritual among you, a strange thing, but true. The soul which looks on God sees him as though she alone were looked on by him. It is in this confidence that she says he is concerned for her, and she for him, and she sees nothing but herself and him. How good you are, LORD, to the soul who seeks you.[10] You come to meet her, you embrace her, you acknowledge yourself to be her Bridegroom,[11] you who are the Lord, God blessed for ever above all things.

— Excerpt from *On the Song of Songs,* Sermon 69:7–8

XIX

Desiring the Beloved's Return

You ask then how I knew he was present, when his ways can in no way be traced?[1] He is life and power,[2] and as soon as he enters in, he awakens my slumbering soul; he stirs and soothes and pierces my heart,[3] for before it was hard as stone,[4] and diseased. So he has begun to pluck out and destroy, to build up and to plant, to water dry places and illuminate dark ones;[5] to open what was closed and to warm what was cold; to make the crooked straight and the rough places smooth,[6] so that my soul may bless the LORD, and all that is within me may praise his holy name.[7] So when the Bridegroom, the Word, came to me, he never made known his coming by any signs, not by sight, not by sound, not by touch. It was not by any movement of his that I recognized his coming; it was not by any of my senses that I perceived he had penetrated to the depths of my being. Only by the movement of my heart, as I have told you, did I perceive his presence; and I knew the power of his might[8] because my faults were put to flight and my human yearnings brought into subjection. I have marveled at the depth of his wisdom[9] when my secret faults[10] have been revealed and made visible; at the very slightest amendment of my way of life I have experienced his goodness and mercy; in the renewal and remaking of the spirit of my mind,[11] that is of my inmost being, I have perceived the excellence of his glorious beauty,[12] and when I contemplate all these things I am filled with awe and wonder at his manifold greatness.[13]

But when the Word has left me, all these spiritual powers become weak and faint and begin to grow cold, as though you had removed the fire from under a boiling pot, and this is the sign of his going. Then my soul must needs be sorrowful[14] until he returns, and my heart again kindles within me[15]—the sign of his returning. When I have had such experience of the Word, is it any wonder that I take to myself the words of the Bride, calling him back when he has withdrawn? For although my fervor is not as strong as hers, yet I am transported by a desire like hers. As long seeking to quench a little the fire of the love she endures, gives no thought to her words or the manner of her speech, but impelled by love she does not speak clearly, but bursts out with whatever comes into her mouth. How should she not do so when she is thus refreshed and satisfied?

— Excerpt from *On the Song of Songs*, Sermon 67:3

as I live the word "return," the word of recall for the recall of the Word, will be on my lips.

As often as he slips away from me, so often shall I call him back. From the burning desire of my heart I will not cease to call him, begging him to return,[16] as if after someone who is departing,[17] and I will implore him to give back to me the joy of his salvation,[18] and restore himself to me.

— Excerpt from *On the Song of Songs*, Sermon 74:6–7

XX

In Search of the Beloved

"In my bed night after night I sought him whom my soul loves."[1] The Bridegroom has not returned when the Bride calls him back with cries and prayers. Why not? He wishes to increase her desire, test her affection, and exercise her faculty of love. He is not displeased with her, he is concealing his love. But he has been sought for, and we must ask whether he may be found, for he did not come when he was called. Yet the Lord said, "Everyone who looks finds";[2] and the words used to recall him were "Return, my beloved, like a roe or a fawn."[3] When he did not return at this call, for the reasons I have given, then she who loved him became more eager and devoted herself eagerly and entirely to seeking him. First she sought him in her bed, but she found him not at all. Then she arose and wandered through the city, going to and fro among the streets and squares,[4] but she did not meet him or catch sight of him.[5] She questions everyone she meets, but there is no news; nor is this search and this disappointment confined to one night or one street, for she says, "I sought him night after night."[6] How great must be her longing and her ardor, that she does not blush to rise in the night and be seen running through the city, questioning everyone openly about her beloved, not to be deflected for any reason from her search for him, undaunted by any obstacle, undeterred by any desire for rest, or by a Bride's modesty, or by terrors of the night![7] Yet in all this she is still disappointed of her hope.[8] Why? What is the reason for this long, unrelenting disappointment, which induces weariness, foments suspicion, inflames impatience, acts as a stepmother to love and a mother to despair? If he is still concealing his love, it is too painful.

Perhaps this concealment may have had some good purpose for a time, until everything was concentrated on calling him, or recalling him. But now she is seeking him and calling for him; what then can be the purpose of any further concealment? If these are incidents in a human marriage, and the love spoken of is physical love, as a superficial reading might imply, then I must leave the matter to those it concerns;[9] but if my task is to give an answer which will satisfy, as far as I can, the minds and affections of those who seek the Lord, then I must draw from Holy Scripture—in which they trust that life to be found[10]—something of vital spiritual importance, that the poor may eat and be satisfied and their hearts may live.[11] And wherein is the life of their hearts but in Jesus my Lord, of whom one who lived in him said, "When Christ our life shall appear, you also will appear with him in glory"?[12] Let him come into our midst so that it may be truly said to us, "One stands among you whom you do not know."[13]

I do not know how the Bridegroom, who is Spirit, can fail to be recognized by spiritual men, who have made sufficient progress in the spirit to say with the prophet, "The LORD's Anointed is the spirit of life to us,"[14] and with the Apostle, "If we think of Christ in a worldly way, we do not know him."[15] Is it not he whom the Bride was seeking? Truly he is the Bridegroom, both loving and lovable. Truly, I tell you, he is the Bridegroom, and his flesh is truly food and his blood truly drink;[16] he is wholly and truly himself, since he is none other than truth itself.[17]

— Excerpt from *On the Song of Songs,* Sermon 75:1–2

XXI

The Secret of the Bridegroom

"Have you seen him whom my soul loves?"[1] O strong and burning love, O love urgent and impetuous, which does not allow me to think of anything but you, you reject all else, you spurn all else but yourself, you are contented only with yourself! You throw order into confusion, ignore moderation; you laugh[2] at all considerations of fitness, reason, modesty, and prudence, and tread them underfoot.[3] All the Bride's thoughts and words are full of nothing but your music and fragrance, so completely have you taken possession of her heart and tongue. "Have you seen him whom my soul loves?" she asks—as though they would know what she meant. Who is it whom your soul loves, for whom you inquire? Has he no name? Who are you and who is he? I speak like this because of the strange manner of speech and extraordinary disregard for names, quite different from the rest of the Scriptures. But in this marriage-song it is not the words which are to be pondered, but the affections behind them. Why is this, except because the sacred love which is the subject of the whole canticle cannot be described in the words of any language, but are expressed in deed and truth?[4] And love speaks everywhere; if anyone desires to grasp these writings, let him love. It is vain for anyone who does not love to listen to this song of love, or to read it, for a cold heart cannot catch fire from its eloquence.[5] The man who does not know Greek cannot understand Greek, nor can anyone without Latin understand someone speaking Latin, and so on. So, too, the language of love will be meaningless jangle to one who does not love, like sounding brass or tinkling cymbal.[6] But as they—I mean the watchmen—have received from the Spirit[7] the desire to love, they know what the Spirit says, and as they understand the expressions of love, they are ready to reply in similar terms, that is, in loving zeal and works of mercy.

This charity would be unbelievable, but that the words of the Bride herself compel belief. For you will observe that she said she wished to bring him whom she held not only to her mother's house but into her bedchamber, which is a mark of singular privilege. For him to enter the house would be enough for salvation; but the privacy of her bedchamber betokens grace, "This day has salvation come to this house,"[8] said our Lord. Salvation must necessarily come to a house once the Savior has entered it. But she who is found worthy to receive him in the bedchamber has a secret for herself alone. Salvation is for the house; the bridal chamber has its own secret delights.[9] "I will bring him to my mother's house,"[10] she says. What house is this, unless it is the one foreshadowed to the Jews. "Behold, your house shall be left for you desolate."[11] He has done what he said, and you have his words in the writings of the prophet: "I have left my house and my inheritance,"[12] and now she promises to bring him back and restore its lost salvation to her mother's house. And if this is not enough, hear the promise of good things which she adds: "and into the bedchamber of her who bore me."[13] He who enters the bridal chamber is the Bridegroom. How great is the power of love! The Savior had left his house and his inheritance in anger; now he has relented and inclined toward her in love, and thus returns not only as Savior but as Bridegroom. You are blessed by the LORD, O daughter,[14] for you have softened his anger and restored the inheritance! You are blessed by your mother, for it is through your blessing that his anger is turned away and salvation restored with him who says "I am your salvation."[15] Nor is this enough. He goes on to say, "I will betrothe you to myself in justice and righteousness; I will betrothe you to myself in mercy and pity."[16] But remember that it is the Bride who has brought about this reconciliation. How can she give up her Bridegroom to another, and choose to do it willingly? But it is not so. She is a good daughter, and desires to share him with her mother, not to give him up. The one is enough for both, for they are one in him.[17] He is our peace,[18] he who made both one, that there might be one Bride and one Bridegroom, Jesus Christ our Lord, who is God above all, blessed for ever. Amen.[19]

— Excerpts from *On the Song of Songs*, Sermon 79:1, 6

XXII

The Fountain of Love

What is more desirable than charity, by whose operation, O soul, not content with a human master, you approach the Word with confidence, cling to him with constancy, speak to him as to a familiar friend, and refer to him in every matter with an intellectual grasp proportionate to the boldness of your desire? Truly this is a spiritual contract, a holy marriage. It is more than a contract, it is an embrace: an embrace where identity of will makes of two one spirit.[1] There need be no fear that inequality of persons should impair the conformity of will, because love is no respecter of persons. It is from loving, not revering, that love receives its name. Let someone filled with horror or stupor or fear or wonder be content with reverence; where there is love all these are unimportant. Love is sufficient for itself; when love is present it absorbs and conquers all other affections. Therefore it loves what it loves, and it knows nothing else. He who is justly honored, held in awe, and admired, prefers to be loved. He and the soul are Bridegroom and Bride. What other bond or compulsion do you look for between those who are betrothed, except to love and be loved?

Rightly, then, does she renounce all other affections and devote herself to love alone, for it is in returning love that she has the power to respond to love. Although she may pour out her whole self in love, what is that compared to the inexhaustible fountain of his love? The stream of love does not flow equally from her who loves and from him who is love, the soul and the Word, the Bride and the Bridegroom, the Creator and the creature—any more than a thirsty man can be compared to a fountain. Will the Bride's vow perish, then because of this? Will the desire of her heart, her burning love, her affirmation of confidence, fail in their purpose because she has not the strength to keep pace with a giant, or rival honey in sweetness, the lamb in gentleness, or the lily in whiteness? Because she cannot equal the brightness of the sun, and the charity of him who is Charity?[2] No. Although the creature loves less, being a lesser being, yet if it loves with its whole heart[3] nothing is lacking, for it has given all. Such love, as I have said, is marriage, for a soul cannot love like this and not be beloved; complete and perfect marriage consists in the exchange of love. No one can doubt that the soul is first loved, and loved more intensely, by the Word; for it is anticipated and surpassed in its love. Happy the soul who is permitted to be anticipated in blessedness so sweet![4] Happy the soul who has been allowed to experience the embrace of such bliss!

— Excerpts from *On the Song of Songs,* Sermon 83:3, 6

XXIII

Found in God

"I sought him whom my soul loves"[1]—this is what you are urged to do by the goodness of him who anticipates you, who sought him, and loved you before you loved him.[2] You would not seek him or love him unless you had first been sought and loved. Not only in one blessing[3] have you been forestalled but in two, being loved as well as being sought. For the love is the reason for the search, and the search is the fruit of the love, and its certain proof. You are loved so that you may not suppose you are sought to be punished. You are sought so that you may not complain you are loved in vain. Both these loving and manifest favors give you courage, and drive away your diffidence, persuading you to return, and stirring your affections. From this comes the zeal and ardor to seek him whom your soul loves,[4] because you cannot seek unless you are sought, and when you are sought you cannot but seek.

Do not forget whence you came. Now, that I may take the words to myself[5]—which is the safest course—is it not you, my soul, who left your first husband,[6] with whom it went well with you, and cast aside your loyalty[7] by going after lovers?[8] And now that you have chosen to commit fornication with them and have been cast aside by them, do you have the effrontery, the insolence, to return to him whom you spurned in your arrogance? Do you seek the light when you are only fit to be hidden, and run to the Bridegroom when you are more deserving of blows than of embraces? It will be a wonder if you do not meet the judge rather than the Bridegroom. Happy the person who hears his soul replying to these reproaches, "I do not fear, because I love; and I could not love at all if I were not loved; therefore this is love." One who is loved has nothing to fear. Let those fear who do not love; they must always live in fear of retribution. Since I love, I cannot doubt that I am loved, any more than I can doubt that I love. Nor can I fear to look on his face, since I have sensed his tenderness. In what have I known it? In this—not only has he sought me as I am, but he has shown me tenderness, and caused me to seek him with confidence. How can I not respond to him when he seeks me, since I respond to him in tenderness? How can he be angry with me for seeking him, when he overlooked the contempt I showed for him? He will not drive away someone who seeks him, when he sought someone who spurned him. The spirit of the Word is gentle,[9] and brings me gentle greetings, speaking to me persuasively of the zeal and desire of the Word, which cannot be hidden from him.[10] He searches the deep things of God,[11] and knows his thoughts—thoughts of peace and not of vengeance.[12] How can I fail to be inspired to seek him, when I have experienced his mercy and been assured of his peace?

Brothers, to realize this is to be taught by the Word; to be convinced of it is to be found.

— Excerpt from *On the Song of Songs,* Sermon 84:5–7

Notes

Foreword

1. Dante Alighieri and translated by Henry Wadsworth Longfellow. *The Divine Comedy, Paradiso*, 32:1.

2. Ibid., Canto XXXII.

I

An Invitation to Love

1. See Rom 1:14.

2. Ps 116:12.

3. See Job 9:3.

4. 1 Cor 13:5.

II

Enduring Love

1. See Mt 17:4.

2. Ps 26:8.

3. Rev 6:9.

4. Lk 15:22.

5. Ps 27:4.

6. See Rom 12:2.

7. See Lk 1:78.

8. See Jer 29:11.

9. See Is 33:6.

10. Song 3:4.

11. See Eph 3:18.

III

The Kiss of the Lord

1. Song 1:1.

2. Rev 2:17.

3. See Sir 24:20.

4. Song 4:12.

5. See 2 Tm 3:6.

6. See Ps 95:6.

7. See Is 35:3.

8. Lam 4:20.

9. See 1 Cor 16:20.

10. See 1 Cor 6:17.

11. Ps 27:8.

12. See Ps 86:4.

13. See Ps 16:11.

IV

An Intimate Love

1. Song 1:1.

2. Gen 2:24.

3. See Ps 45:11.

4. See Mt 12:34.

5. Ps 73:25.

6. See Ps 104:32.

7. See Song 1:3; 2:4.

8. Ps 36:9.

9. See 1 Jn 4:18.

V

The Spirit of Love

1. Sir 3:22.

2. See Gal 5:16.

3. See Song 3:1.

4. See 1 Cor 8:1.

5. See Rom 10:2.

6. Ps 45:2.

7. Ps 19:2.

8. See Rom 11:34.

VI

Rest in God

1. Song 1:1.

2. See Ps 99:4.

3. See Titus 2:12.

4. See Is 38:15.

5. See Phil 3:6.

6. See Titus 3:1.

7. See Gen 3:19.

8. See Hos 10:11.

9. See Lk 17:10.

10. Ps 143:6.

11. See See Ps 20:4.

12. See Is 11:2.

13. Ps 63:5.

14. Ps 71:8.

15. Ps 31:19.

VII

The Touch of the Lord

1. See Lk 24:19.

2. See Gen 18:27.

3. See Job 21:24.

4. See Is 66:14.

5. See Eccl 4:12.

6. See Rom 5:10.

7. See Gen 2:7.

8. See 1 Cor 15:45.

9. See Titus 2:7.

10. See Prov 31:19.

11. See Ps 144:1.

12. See Wis 8:1.

13. See Jer 17:14.

14. See Ps 7:17.

15. Song 1:3.

16. See Ps 143:2.

17. See Ps 103:4.

18. See Phil 2:9.

19. See Dan 3:52.

20. See Ps 104:15.

21. See Ps 141:5; Mt 6:17.

22. See Is 62:2.

23. Lk 2:21.

24. See Joel 2:32.

25. See Rom 1:25.

VIII

The Wonder of God's Love

1. See Ps 35:1.

2. See Ps 16:8.

3. Ps 104:33; 146:2.

4. See Ps 78:4.

5. Lk 1:52–53.

6. Mt 22:39; Jn 9:39.

7. Ps 119:52.

8. See Lam 3:40.

9. See Jn 14:17.

10. See Jn 15:5.

11. Ps 78:39.

12. See 2 Cor 3:18.

13. See Ps 18:28.

14. See Eph 5:8.

15. See Sermon 16:1.

16. See Ps 111:10.

17. See Phil 1:11.

18. See Rom 1:25.

IX

The Right Kind of Love

1. 1 Cor 16:22.

2. See Ps 144:3.

3. Eccl 12:13.

4. See Is 38:10.

5. See Ps 51:17.

6. See Ps 102:11.

7. See Is 38:15.

8. See Ps 38:9.

9. See Ps 69:6.

10. See Ps 33:9; 148:5.

11. See 1 Cor 1:24.

12. Deut 6:5.

13. Song 8:6.

X

In the Room of the King

1. Ps 103:17.

2. Ps 119:63.

3. See Rom 8:28.

4. Ps 32:2.

5. Rom 3:23.

6. Rom 8:33.

7. See Ps 51:6.

8. 1 Jn 5:18.

9. See Eph 1:16; 1:4.

10. See Ps 63:3.

11. See Rom 8:29.

12. See 1 Pet 4:8.

13. Ps 32:1.

14. See Deut 32:10.

15. See Ps 106:4–5.

16. See Rom 12:2.

17. Song 1:4.

XI

The Capacity for God

1. See Ps 46:11.

2. Wis 1:4.

3. 2 Cor 6:13.

4. Eph 4:13.

5. Eph 2:21.

6. 1 Cor 13:2.

7. See Lk 6:32.

8. See Mt 5:47.

9. See Phil 4:15.

10. See Mt 5:47.

11. See Mt 19:19.

12. Rom 13:8.

13. See Mt 11:12.

14. See 1 Jn 3:17.

15. See Mt 5:44.

16. See Ps 120:7.

17. Ps 104:2.

XII

A Face-to-Face Encounter

1. See Rom 1:20.

2. Mt 9:12.

3. Lk 24:32.

4. Song 1:3.

5. Lk 15:17.

6. See Song 1:4.

7. Prov 31:11.

8. Mt 28:20.

XIII

Athirst for God

1. See Ps 73:28.

2. See Dan 9:23.

3. See Phil 1:23.

4. See 1 Pet 5:6.

5. See Ps 21:3.

6. See 2 Cor 5:6.

7. See Ps 21:3.

8. See Rev 14:4.

9. See Ps 93:1.

10. Job 10:1–2.

11. See Jas 1:14.

12. See Ps 45:8.

13. Ps 147:3.

14. Is 61:1.

15. Mt 9:13.

XIV

Alone with God

1. See Lam 4:20.

2. See Mt 6:6.

3. See Lk 6:12; 9:18.

4. See Jn 12:36.

5. See Mt 26:37.

6. See Lk 10:37; 22:41.

7. See 2 Sam 19:19.

8. See Rom 1:25.

XV

A Loving Affirmation

1. Song 1:15.

2. See Juvenal, *Satires* 6:165.

3. See 1 Cor 4:4.

4. See Job 13:26.

5. Song 1:13.

6. See 1 Cor 2:2.

7. Gen 22:12.

8. See Song 1:14.

XVI

The Embrace of God

1. Song 2:5.

2. See Mt 25:5.

3. See Jer 2:13.

4. See Lk 8:6.

5. See Ps 67:10.

6. See Is 61:11.

7. See 2 Cor 9:10.

8. See 1 Cor 13:5.

9. See Phil 3:7.

10. Song 2:6.

11. See Jn 13:25.

XVII

Aflame with Holy Love

1. Song 2:16.

2. See Jn 16:18.

3. See Jn 10:24.

4. See Is 24:16.

5. Lk 6:45.

XVIII

Confidence in the Love of God

1. Song 2:16.

2. See 1 Cor 7:32.

3. Mt 7:2.

4. Song 2:16.

5. See 2 Cor 3:18.

6. Ps 18:26.

7. Prov 8:17.

8. See Lam 2:19.

9. See Ps 77:5.

10. See Lam 3:25.

11. See Rom 9:5.

XIX

Desiring the Beloved's Return

1. See Rom 11:33.

2. See Heb 4:12.

3. See Song 4:9.

4. See Sir 3:27; Ezek 11:19.

5. See Cf. Jer 1:10.

6. See Is 40:4.

7. See Ps 103:1.

8. See Eph 1:13.

9. See Eccl 7:25.

10. See Ps 19:13.

11. See Eph 4:13.

12. See Ps 50:2.

13. See Ps 150:2.

14. See Mt 26:33; Ps 42:6, 12; Ps 43:5.

15. See Ps 109:22.

16. See Ps 21:3.

17. See Judg 18:23.

18. See Ps 51:14.

XX

In Search of the Beloved

1. Song 3:1.

2. Mt 7:8.

3. Song 2:17.

4. See Song 3:1–2.

5. See Song 3:3.

6. Song 3:1.

7. See Ps 90:5.

8. See Ps 77:30.

9. See Acts 18:15.

10. See Jn 5:39.

11. See Ps 21:27.

12. Col 3:4.

13. Jn 1:26.

14. Lam 4:20.

15. 2 Cor 5:16.

16. See Jn 6:56.

17. See Jn 14:6.

XXI

The Secret of the Bridegroom

1. Song 3:3.

2. See Col 2:15.

3. See 2 Cor 10:5.

4. See 1 Jn 3:18.

5. See Ps 118:140.

6. See 1 Cor 3:1.

7. See Jn 7:39.

8. Lk 19:9.

9. See Is 24:16.

10. Song 3:4.

11. Lk 13:35.

12. Jer 12:7.

13. Song 3:4.

14. See Jdt 13:23.

15. Ps 34:3.

16. Hos 2:20.

17. See Mt 19:56.

18. See Eph 2:14.

19. See Rom 9:5.

XXII

The Fountain of Love

1. See 1 Cor 6:17.

2. See 1 Jn 4:16.

3. See Mt 22:37.

4. See Ps 21:4.

XXIII

Found in God

1. Song 3:1.

2. See 1 Jn 4:10.

3. See Gen 27:28.

4. See Song 3:1.

5. See 1 Cor 4:6.

6. See Sir 23:22.

7. See 1 Tim 5:12.

8. See Hos 2:5, 13.

9. See Wis 1:6.

10. See Mt 5:14.

11. See 1 Cor 2:10.

12. See Jer 29:11.

Bibliography

Bernard of Clairvaux. *Five Books on Consideration: Advice to a Pope.* Translated by John D. Anderson and Elizabeth T. Kennan. Kalamazoo, MI: Cistercian Publications, 1976.

———. *On Loving God.* Translated by Robert Walton. Washington, D.C.: Cistercian Publications, 1974.

———. *On the Song of Songs I.* Translated by Kilian Walsh. Spencer, MA: Cistercian Publications, 1971.

———. *On the Song of Songs II.* Translated by Kilian Walsh. Kalamazoo, MI: Cistercian Publications, 1976.

———. *On the Song of Songs III.* Translated by Kilian Walsh and Irene M. Edmonds. Kalamazoo, MI: Cistercian Publications, 1979.

———. *On the Song of Songs IV.* Translated by Irene Edmonds. Kalamazoo, MI: Cistercian Publications, 1980.

Dante, Alighieri. *The Divine Comedy, Paradiso.* Translated by Henry Wadsworth Longfellow. Boston, MA: Ticknor and Fields, 1867.

BOOKS & MEDIA

The Daughters of St. Paul operate book and media centers at the following addresses. Visit, call, or write the one nearest you today, or find us at www.pauline.org.

CALIFORNIA

3908 Sepulveda Blvd, Culver City, CA 90230	310-397-8676
935 Brewster Avenue, Redwood City, CA 94063	650-369-4230
5945 Balboa Avenue, San Diego, CA 92111	858-565-9181

FLORIDA

145 S.W. 107th Avenue, Miami, FL 33174	305-559-6715

HAWAII

1143 Bishop Street, Honolulu, HI 96813	808-521-2731
Neighbor Islands call:	866-521-2731

ILLINOIS

172 North Michigan Avenue, Chicago, IL 60601	312-346-4228

LOUISIANA

4403 Veterans Memorial Blvd, Metairie, LA 70006	504-887-7631

MASSACHUSETTS

885 Providence Hwy, Dedham, MA 02026	781-326-5385

MISSOURI

9804 Watson Road, St. Louis, MO 63126	314-965-3512

NEW YORK

64 W. 38th Street, New York, NY 10018	212-754-1110

PENNSYLVANIA

Philadelphia—relocating	215-676-9494

SOUTH CAROLINA

243 King Street, Charleston, SC 29401	843-577-0175

VIRGINIA

1025 King Street, Alexandria, VA 22314	703-549-3806

CANADA

3022 Dufferin Street, Toronto, ON M6B 3T5	416-781-9131

¡También somos su fuente para libros,
videos y música en español!